ONE steep, snowy slope.

TWO mountain peaks stand above the snowy slope.

THREE skiers ride
a lift to the top
of the snowy slope.

three
3
•••

3

4

FOUR sledders jump on a toboggan at the top of the snowy slope.

FIVE snowboarders ride and race down the snowy slope.

five
5
• • • • •

8

SIX ski poles lean on a fence at the top of the snowy slope.

six
6

SEVEN pairs of boots keep feet warm on the snowy slope.

eight

8

EIGHT tracks in the snow weave down the snowy slope.

NINE flags flutter
in the wind
along the snowy slope.

TEN round, humpy bumps
        jut out of the snowy slope.

ten
10

ELEVEN sturdy trees block the way at the bottom of the snowy slope.

TWELVE stars
silently shine high above
the snowy slope.

21

Fun Facts

 Alpine skiing is another name for downhill skiing. The word *Alpine* comes from the word *Alps*, which are the mountains in Europe where skiing started.

 Many ski areas use round tubes instead of toboggans for people to ride down the slopes.

 A snowboard is more than two times wider but a little shorter than a ski.

 About three inches from the bottom of the ski pole is a round or star-shaped piece of plastic. This keeps the pole from sinking too far into the snow.

 A springy binding holds the boot in place on the ski. If a skier falls, the bindings let the boots come off the skis so the skier's legs won't be hurt.

 The special mounds or bumps on a ski slope are called moguls.

Find the Numbers

Now you have finished reading the story, but a surprise still awaits you.

Hidden in each picture is one of the numbers from 1 to 12. Can you find them all?

Key

1—toward the bottom right section of snowy slope

2—on the lowest snowy area on the left mountain

3—the connector between the center chair and rope

4—on the child's blue boot

5—on the front of the red snowboard

6—the strap on the farthest left ski pole

7—on the boot of the skier who is farthest left

8—on the hair of the skier who is farthest right

9—on the ski pole of the skier who is farthest right

10—on the skier's left glove

11—on the door

12—above the door

Go on an Observation Walk

Counting is fun! Step outside your door, and practice counting by going on an observation walk in your neighborhood—or even in your own yard. Ask an adult to go with you. On an observation walk, you notice the things all around you. Count the number of trees in your yard or on your block. Count the number of dogs you see. Count the number of windows on one side of your home. You can count everything!

Glossary

flutter—flap quickly

peak—the pointed top of a mountain

slope—a trail used for skiing down a mountain

toboggan—a long sled that curls up in the front

Index

On the Web

Fact Hound
Fact Hound offers a safe, fun way to find Web sites related to this book. All of the sites on Fact Hound have been researched by our staff.
http://www.facthound.com

1. Visit the Fact Hound home page.

2. Enter a search word related to this book, or type in this special code: 1404805796.

3. Click on the FETCH IT button.

Your trusty Fact Hound will fetch the best sites for you!

Acknowledgments

Thanks to our advisers for their expertise, research, and advice:

Stuart Farm, M.A.
Mathematics Lecturer,
University of North Dakota
Grand Forks, North Dakota

Susan Kesselring, M.A.
Literacy Educator
Rosemount-Apple Valley-Eagan
(Minnesota) School District

The editor would like to thank Sarah May at Vail Resorts for her expert advice in preparing this book.

Managing Editor: Bob Temple
Creative Director: Terri Foley
Editor: Brenda Haugen
Editorial Adviser: Andrea Cascardi
Copy Editor: Sue Gregson
Designer: Nathan Gassman

Page production: Picture Window Books
The illustrations in this book were rendered digitally.

Picture Window Books
5115 Excelsior Boulevard
Suite 232
Minneapolis, MN 55416
1-877-845-8392
www.picturewindowbooks.com

Library of Congress Cataloging-in-Publication Data
Dahl, Michael.
Downhill fun : a counting book about winter / written by Michael Dahl ; illustrated by Todd Ouren.
p. cm. — (Know your numbers)
Summary: Introduces the numbers from one to twelve as skiers, sledders, and snowboarders whiz down a snowy slope. Readers are invited to find hidden numbers on an illustrated activity page. Includes bibliographical references and index.
ISBN 1-4048-0579-6 (reinforced library binding)
1. Winter sports—Juvenile literature. 2. Counting—Juvenile literature.
[1. Winter sports. 2. Counting. 3. Picture puzzles.]
I. Ouren, Todd, ill.
II. Title.
GV841.15 .D35 2004
796.9—dc22
2003020941